THE YANKEE FAN'S
LITTLE BOOK OF WISDOM

Also available from Diamond Communications:

New Editions:

The Cubs Fan's Little Book of Wisdom by Jim Langford

The Red Sox Fan's Little Book of Wisdom by Curt Smith

The Cardinals Fan's Little Book of Wisdom by Rob Rains

The Yankees Fan's Little Book of Wisdom by George Sullivan

The Giants Fan's Little Book of Wisdom by David D'Antonio

THE YANKEES FAN'S
LITTLE BOOK OF WISDOM

Centennial Edition

George Sullivan

Diamond Communications
A Member of the Rowman & Littlefield Publishing Group
Lanham • South Bend • New York • Oxford

THE YANKEES FAN'S LITTLE BOOK OF WISDOM
Copyright © 2002 by George Sullivan

Manufactured in the United States of America

Published by Diamond Communications
An imprint of The Rowman & Littlefield Publishing Group, Inc.
4501 Forbes Boulevard, Suite 200
Lanham, Maryland 20706
Distributed by NATIONAL BOOK NETWORK
1-800-462-6420

ISBN 1-888698-51-9 (pbk. : alk. paper)

For two more winners:

Brian Guittarr, with a grandfather's love . . .

And Casey Stengel, who was unfailingly gracious to a 15-year-old bat boy at Fenway Park when he didn't have to be. As Wes Westrum once malapropped of Casey, "Boy, when they made him, they threw away the molding."

"The name Yankees *stands for something all over the world."*

—Charles Dillon Stengel, who also told his players,
"You're the Yankees—the *best*."

Realize some things are more important than baseball.

As the Yankees learned after September 11, 2001.

Know when to leave well enough alone.

"Baseball is a kid's game," manager Bob Lemon once said, "that grown-ups only tend to screw up."

Take pleasure in whatever you do.

"If you're not having fun in baseball,"
Chris Chambliss said, "you miss the point of everything."

Inspiration is all around us.

Look no further than southpaw Jim Abbott, born with one arm,
who no-hit the Cleveland Indians at the Stadium in 1993.

Beware of know-it-alls.

"When you think you know baseball, you don't," Yogi Berra has said.
He also said, "In baseball, you don't know *nothing*."

Some things change . . .

Jason Giambi makes more in *one game* (over $105,000) than Mickey Mantle ever did in a *year* ($100,000 tops). And Giambi makes as much in *1.5 official at-bats* as Lou Gehrig did in a *season* (about $40,000 at most). Finally, consider this: Giambi makes far more in *one trip to the plate* than the $18,000 the franchise cost in 1903 when New Yorkers Frank Farrell and Big Bill Devery purchased the ailing Baltimore Orioles and transplanted them in Manhattan.

. . . and some things don't.

Wee Willie Keeler was the franchise's first hero after jumping the
National League for a record $10,000 (a staggering $71.50 per game).
"I am in baseball for all I can get out of it," explained the Brooklyn
native, who jilted his hometown nine to cross the East River.
"In baseball, as in any profession, business prevails over sentiment.
. . . Sentiment don't go when the coin is to be considered. . . .
Who remembers a ballplayer after he gets through with the game?
I'm a philosopher, I am, and believe in the good old coin."

Dreams come true
for those who persist.

"All I've ever wanted to be is a Yankee," Derek Jeter says.
"When I was a kid, I was always hoping there'd be a jersey left for me
to wear with a single digit, because of all the retired numbers."

"Do as I say, not as I do" happens.

"Goddamn it, stop that goddamn swearing over there!"
Babe Ruth once scolded while lecturing a cluster of young fans.

Choose words carefully.

"He's not moody," Sparky Lyle corrected a description
of sour pal and batterymate Thurman Munson.
"Moody means you're nice some of the time."

Appreciate yourself—
within reason.

"Sometimes," Reggie Jackson once admired,
"I can't even appreciate the magnitude of me."

Never trust a pitcher with a bat in his hands.

Like Roger Clemens. Ask fellow New Yorker Mike Piazza.

Some matters eclipse baseball.

"The biggest game I ever pitched," Orlando Hernandez has said,
"was when I jumped on a raft and left Cuba."

Despise losing . . .

Like George Steinbrenner, who has said,
"I hate to lose. Hate, hate, hate to lose."

. . . but understand you need not win 'em all.

As Casey Stengel once pointed out, "The Yankees don't pay me to win every day—just two out of three."

16

Like 'em or not, sportswriters can be constructive.

New York Press sports editor Jim Price, weary of trying to squeeze "Highlanders" into headlines, rechristened them the "Yankees" in spring 1913—and it stuck.

Always be prepared.

As was bench coach Don Zimmer, when he donned a soldier's helmet (complete with *NY* logo) in the dugout after being bloodied by Chuck Knoblauch's foul liner off the ear during the previous night's 1999 division series opener.

Loyalty has limits.

"I'm a Mets fan now," reacted Joann Barrett,
34 and pregnant, after being shot in the hand during
a July 4, 1985, game at Yankee Stadium.

(Police couldn't find the spent bullet—
until it was discovered in her handbag two days later.)

Some people just don't grasp the team concept.

Like Ruben Sierra, an individualist who spat
at the Yankees after being shipped to Detroit during
the 1996 season, "All they care about is winning."

There always will be some who envy you.

"Hating the Yankees," Chicago-based columnist Mike Royko once wrote, "is as American as pizza pie, unwed mothers, and cheating on your income tax."

It ain't braggin' if it's the truth.

As Paul O'Neill said in 2000, after the Yanks had won yet another World Series, "If you're a Yankee fan, or if you're not a Yankee fan, you have to admit—we're winners."

Thinking can be hazardous.

"When you start thinking is when you
get your ass beat," Sparky Lyle noted.

Be versatile;
diversify your interests.

Bernie Williams not only stars as a two-way talent for the Yankees
but is an accomplished classical guitarist.

Be dedicated.

"So I eat, drink and sleep baseball 24 hours a day," manager
Joe McCarthy once remarked. "What's wrong with that?"

Some things moms just don't understand.

When comedian/actor/Yankee enthusiast Billy Crystal informed his mother that he had just purchased Mickey Mantle's old glove at auction for "a quarter-million dollars," she responded, "What was wrong with the glove we bought you at Davega's?"

Some wives *tell* it like it is . . .

"I'm 43 and I'm still married to a 4-year-old," Anita Piniella
told hot-tempered husband Lou after learning of the
Yankee manager's latest tantrum on the diamond.

. . . and some just take action.

As Mickey Rivers' wife reportedly did. Unhappy with her husband
about something or other, she repeatedly plowed her car
into his in the players' parking lot at the Stadium.

Nothing is hopeless.

As columnist Jim Murray used to say: "When you think everything is hopeless, just remember Yogi Berra."

No question is a silly question. Or is it?

"What do you fellows think I am," millionaire owner Jacob Ruppert would tell his Yankees seeking raises, "a millionaire?"

Sign autographs carefully.

Remember that shapely Chicago blonde who mooned the 1979 Yankees' bus outside old Comiskey Park three days in a row—before slipping aboard and reportedly collecting autographs on her bared behind?

31

Know thyself.

"I could never be a manager," Mickey Mantle once said.
"I can't manage myself. What would I do with 25 other problems?"

Don't expect rewards—
even after giving your all
in 2,130 consecutive games.

Dying Lou Gehrig, who didn't suit up the last two years of his
1935–1941 captaincy, reportedly wasn't paid those two seasons.

At least the Ironman had the Yankee loving cup presented on
memorable Lou Gehrig Day 1939. Estimated worth: $5

Plan carefully.

The Yankees' 1975 "Army Day," celebrating the Armed Forces'
200th birthday, proved memorable. The ceremony's climax was
a thundering barrage—which shredded windows and blew away
part of the center-field fence at Shea Stadium (where the team
was playing while Yankee Stadium was being renovated).

Some things can't be understood.

"The Yankees are only interested in one thing," two-tour Yankee Luis Polonia was once quoted, "and I don't know what it is."

Know your anatomy.

"Just because your legs is dead doesn't mean your head is, too,"
Casey Stengel advised when fired by the Yankees at age 70.

Know you can be ruled wrong even when you are right.

George Brett's controversial "pine tar" home run at the Stadium proved that—costing the Yankees a 1983 victory.

Know you can be ruled right even when it appears wrong.

The Yankees seemingly lost, 10–9, on Don Money's ninth-inning bases-full homer at Milwaukee in 1976. But just before Sparky Lyle delivered the pitch, Chris Chambliss requested time out—which was granted by first-base ump Jim McKean, nullifying the slam. Money then fanned, and the pinstripers escaped.

38

There's no place like home— even on the road.

Unhappy with the visiting-team locker-room accomodations at Shea Stadium during the 2000 Subway Series, George Steinbrenner had his team's home clubhouse furniture trucked over from Yankee Stadium— providing his players with the comforts of home.

Tobacco is never good for you.

As Steve Hamilton attests. The southpaw swallowed his chaw
while pitching—and promptly vomited on the mound.

Be a trendsetter.

The 1929 Yankees were the first major league
team to wear uniform numbers regularly.

All heroes aren't celebrated.

"My dad was my biggest hero," Derek Jeter says,
"but they haven't made a poster of him yet."

Luck isn't luck at all.

"You make your own luck," Casey Stengel professed. "Some people have bad luck all their lives." Fellow Hall of Famer Branch Rickey, a one-time Yankee catcher, agreed: "Luck is the residue of design."

Do the best you can with what you've got.

"A manager has his cards dealt to him,"
Miller Huggins philosophized, "and he must play them."

History has a way of repeating itself.

As Yogi Berra said after seeing Maris and Mantle smack back-to-back homers time after time, "It's *déjà vu* all over again!"

Blessed are the peacemakers, for they sometimes end up on the disabled list.

Like Bobby Murcer, injured while breaking up a
Rick Dempsey–Bill Sudakis bout in a Milwaukee hotel lobby.

Love thy neighbor.

As Casey Stengel said of prize pupil Billy Martin,
"The fresh little bastard. How I love him."

Love thy neighbor's wife.

Pitchers Fritz Peterson and Mike Kekich exchanged wives
(along with families and pets) in 1973. "It isn't a wife swap,"
Kekich clarified before being banished to Cleveland. "It's a life swap."

When appropriate, issue challenges.

"Sixty, count 'em, *sixty!*" Babe Ruth roared in the Yankees clubhouse while celebrating his record sixtieth home run in the second-to-last game of the 1927 season. "Let's see some other son of a bitch match that!"

Work hard, but have fun.

Like David Wells.

Recognize your own abilities.

"Sang the shit out of it, didn't I?" Robert Merrill
conceded to Red Smith aboard a Yankee Stadium elevator,
when the columnist complimented the world-acclaimed baritone on
his rendition of *The Star Spangled Banner* before a World Series game.

Teams succeed, not individuals.

"We may not have the best players,
but we certainly have the best team," Joe Torre said in
2000 after his Yankees won a third consecutive World Series.

Be careful who you pick on.

Fed up with a New Yorker's taunts, Ty Cobb climbed into
the stands and beat his handicapped tormentor bloody in 1912.
The heckler protested, "Cobb hit me in the face with his fist,
knocked me down, jumped on me, kicked me, spiked me,
and booted me behind the ear." To which Cobb responded,
"I'm pleased I didn't overlook any important punitive measures."

Informed the loudmouth had just one hand
(and only three fingers) from a print-shop accident,
Cobb scowled, "I don't care if he has no feet!"

Safeguard your employees' health and welfare.

That's what George Steinbrenner undoubtedly had in mind
in 1982 when he said of pummeled pitcher Doyle Alexander,
"I'm afraid some of our players might get hurt playing behind him."
(Captain Graig Nettles reacted, "I wasn't worried. Maybe I might
have been if I was sitting in the left-field stands.")

As Yogi said, "Ninety percent of this game is half mental."

Remember Chuck Knoblauch throwing
the ball from second base? Or trying to.

Always get a kick out of the game.

Fiery Norman Elberfeld was the franchise's first shortstop and second
manager. New York fans got a kick out of the colorful "Tabasco Kid,"
and so did an umpire. Elberfeld chased the ump around old Hilltop
Park, kicking at him, until finally restrained by police.

Don't believe all you read . . .

Babe Ruth was reported dead numerous times while a Yankee, including once in "detail" by a British newspaper.

. . . or all you hear.

"Berra swings and hits a high foul behind the plate,"
Phil Rizzuto reported early in his broadcasting career.
"It's coming down . . . and Yogi makes the catch!"

Some winners aren't winners.

Don Mattingly is the only Yankee not to have participated
in a World Series whose number has been retired.

Ironically, the Yankees won the 1996 world championship
the year after popular "Donnie Baseball" quit.

When you do the unexpected, make it count. And do it spectacularly.

Like Derek Jeter and his season-saving play in the 2001 division play-offs. Who can forget when the supershortstop raced across the infield, speared an errant throw from the outfield, then flipped a backhand shovel pass on target to nail the Oakland A's runner at the plate. Crucially, it preserved a 1–0 lead and sparked the two-games-down Yankees to three straight wins and a series victory to keep hopes alive for a fourth consecutive world championship in the Bronx.

Coincidences are a spice of life.

What were the odds that Don Larsen, making a rare appearance back
in Yankee Stadium for Yogi Berra Day in July 1999, would attend
David Cone's perfect game? And what were the chances that Wally
Pipp, Lou Gehrig's predecessor, would be present in Detroit in May
1939 when the Iron Horse ended his 2,130-game playing streak?

Some things take awhile.

It wasn't until Roger Maris' home-run record was
broken four decades later that the late Yankee slugger
got the appreciation and respect he deserved.

Don't hesitate to send a message . . . and don't be intimidated.

Tommy Byrne once threw a warmup pitch at the batter on-deck—
Ted Williams. (Williams often moved from the on-deck circle to
near the plate while a new pitcher took his warmups—the better
to preview his stuff. Byrne, who liked to psyche batters, fired a
pitch past the catcher and close to Ted. "I winged one at him
to run him away from there," Byrne told Donald Honig.
"He didn't appreciate it one bit. I could see him growling.")

It all comes out in the wash.

"How scared was I?" manager Bob Lemon quipped after his Yankees survived the thrilling deciding game of the 1981 playoffs against the Kansas City Royals. "Only my laundryman knows for sure."

Praise the Lord. Always . . .

"I want to thank the Good Lord for making me a Yankee,"
Joe DiMaggio told the overflow of Bronx crowd on his
"day" in 1949.

Current Yankees are reminded of DiMag's words
daily at the Stadium—the saying etched in large lettering
above the runway connecting clubhouse and dugout.

. . . and never hesitate
to seek His help.

A sign posted above teammate Rickey Henderson's locker
by a Yankee wit sniped: "O Lord, help my words to be gracious
and tender today, for tomorrow I may have to eat them."

Don't be talked out of decisions.

When Casey Stengel removed a struggling pitcher
who claimed he wasn't tired, the manager reached
for the ball and explained, "Well, I'm tired of you."

Some things add up.

Jason Giambi chose *25* for his Yankee number—because the digits add up to the *7* retired for Mickey Mantle, his father John's favorite player. "We didn't get *7*, Pops," Jason said upon becoming a Yankee, "but we got the pinstripes."

When all else fails, blame the umpire.

Sour Carl Mays refused any responsibility after his "submarine pitch" skulled Cleveland's Ray Chapman in 1920 at New York, the only fatal pitch in major-league history. Instead, the generally despised Yankee pitcher alibied "it was the umpire's fault" for allowing a scuffed ball to be used. "My conscience is absolutely clear," Mays said.

Know where you are at all times.

Unlike Bob Sheppard, when he made a rare error one summer night
in 1976. After rushing from a Yankees' day game across the Hudson
to the opening of new Giants Stadium that evening, he dashed to
his public-address microphone and announced breathlessly, "Good
evening, ladies and gentlemen, and welcome to Yankee Stadium . . ."

Don't expect everyone to love you.

Essaying on the Yankees–Mets showdown in the
2000 World Series, George Will wrote: "For America west
of the Hudson, the best thing about a Subway Series is that it
guarantees that millions of New York baseball fans—the followers
of whichever team loses—are going to be depressed." Ouch.

And the political columnist suggested another benefit:
"A Subway Series encourages New Yorkers to vent their native
rudeness on each other rather than on the rest of us." Double ouch.

Punch endings can be awesome. Literally.

Ask Bill Bevens. One out from immortality, he lost a no-hitter, and Game 4 of the '47 World Series, on Dodger Cookie Lavagetto's two-run walk-off pinch double at Brooklyn.

Or check with Mickey Owen. One pitch away from a Brooklyn victory in Game 4 of the '41 Series, an apparent game-ending third strike to Tommy Henrich eluded the Dodger catcher—igniting a four-run rally that gave the Yankees a 3–1 lead in the Series, which they clinched the next day.

Know how to deal with the media . . .

"If Reggie (Jackson) felt that a sportswriter was walking past his locker without talking to him," teammate Graig Nettles observed, "he'd trip him."

. . . even when you criticize 'em.

"We're playin' bad every place—not hittin', not pitchin' and not fieldin' too good," Casey Stengel once told the press. "And judgin' by what I read in the newspapers, the Yankee writers are in a slump, too."

Always use logic.

As logical Wee Willie Keeler, the franchise's first gate attraction
and highest paid player at $10,000 per annum, suggested,
"Hit 'em where they ain't"—and did it often enough
to lead the club in batting its first three seasons.

Even the best have bad days.

Like Mariano Rivera, arguably baseball's greatest big-game closer
ever, unraveling in the final half-inning of the 2001 World Series.
After fanning the side in the eighth, putting the Yankees on the thresh-
old of a fourth consecutive world title, Rivera fell apart in the ninth as
Arizona rallied for two runs and a 3–2 victory—and the crown.

Value family values.

"Throw in another hundred and you can take the rest of the family,"
Jumping Joe Dugan's father told the scout who had just forked
over $500 for his teenage son's services back in the Teens.

Baseball is a dirty game.

"If my uniform doesn't get dirty," noted Rickey Henderson, the Yankees' all-time stolen-base king, "I haven't done anything in the baseball game."

There is no such thing as back to the future.

As Yogi Berra said, "The future ain't what it used to be."

Some acts defy comprehension.

Like why a teammate making a million dollars would steal (and then sell) star shortstop Derek Jeter's favorite glove, a fielder's prized tool.

Avoid making David Letterman's Top Ten.

Describing what it is like to be dead, Letterman defined, "It's like listening to New York Yankees announcer Phil Rizzuto during a rain delay."

An honest question deserves an honest answer.

As blunt Thurman Munson replied to batterymate Ron Guidry's "What do you think?" after a shaky first inning: "I think you ought to say a prayer."

Think big . . .

Like Babe Ruth, whose philosophy was simple: "I swing big, with everything I've got. I hit big or I miss big. I like to live as big as I can."

83

. . . and think quickly.

Bobby Murcer stole a homer from Long Islander Carl Yastrzemski at the old Stadium. Ron Woods leaped for a ball, snagged it, and tumbled into the roped-off rightfield stands—KO-ing himself. Racing over from center field, Murcer peered over the low railing and saw the ball next to the unconscious Woods' glove . . . and quickly slipped the ball into the glove a moment before an umpire arrived and called Yaz out.

Think big.

"Hell, if I'd a hit that many singles," Mickey Mantle scorned
Pete Rose's all-time hit mark, "I'd a worn a dress."

Reconciliation is always possible.

Look at Yogi Berra and George Steinbrenner, who didn't speak for
fourteen years before making up in 1999.

Get into the Hall of Fame
any way you can.

Ron Blomberg's bat may be the only one displayed in the Hall of Fame for a base on balls. Blomberg was the majors' first designated hitter, walking with the bases loaded in the 1973 opener at Boston. After visiting his historic bat at Cooperstown, Blomberg told writer Phil Pepe, "It's a funny way to make the Hall of Fame."

Speak only of what you know.

"I can tell you Billy [Martin] has a great heart,"
Whitey Ford said of his pal, "but I can't vouch for his liver."

88

It's true: Ill fortune sometimes comes in threes.

Tommy John made three errors on one play at the Stadium in 1988—bobbling a dribbler to the mound, then overthrowing first base, then cutting off right fielder Dave Winfield's throw and heaving the ball into the third-base dugout. "I think I just lost a Gold Glove on that play," said the 45-year-old southpaw, who won the game anyway, 16–3 (but for the 25th season in a row failed to acquire a Gold Glove).

Don't laugh when the boss says, "Do as I say . . ."

In the mortal words of the immortal George Steinbrenner,
"I've always said that if you wait and keep your mouth shut,
things will come around right."

Keep it simple, stupid.

"Pick a good one and sock it," said Babe Ruth
explaining his power-hitting genius.

Never say never.

"There is absolutely no hope that their organization will be a winning organization as long as Steinbrenner runs the show. . . . It's sad," Dallas Green advised after being canned during his first season managing in the Bronx in 1989—before the Yankees (and George Steinbrenner) launched their string of championships.

Looks can be deceiving . . .

Look at Lawrence Peter Berra. "Talking to Yogi Berra about baseball is like talking to Homer about the gods," noted A. Bartlett Giamatti, one-time classics professor and Yale president who became commissioner of baseball.

. . . but not always.

Remember Hank Bauer, who looked like he'd stepped out
of a Marine Corps recruiting poster with a face that writer
Maury Allen described as "looking like a clenched fist."

94

Speak up, even if you're not always understood.

"Sometimes," Casey Stengel mused, "I get a little hard-of-speaking."

Always set the record straight.

"I really didn't say everything I said," Dr. L. P. "Yogi" Berra,
honorary degree recipient, told graduates in 1996
at New Jersey's Montclair State University.

Don't ask silly questions.

When asked if he considered relieving Bill Stafford when the
pitcher was struck by a liner during the 1962 World Series,
manager Ralph Houk, baseball's iron major, replied,
"No. There wasn't any blood showing, was there?"

Qualifications are required for most jobs.

"Before he writes a book," manager Dallas Green reacted to reports that Rickey Henderson might pen a tell-all book on the Yankees, "he's got to read one."

98

It's true—seeing isn't always believing.

"Someone has to tell me we just beat the New York Yankees and Mariano Rivera, because I still don't believe it," veteran first baseman Mark Grace marvelled after Arizona rallied for two runs in the ninth inning of Game 7 in the 2001 World Series to dethrone the Yankees after three straight world championships.

Even the most marvelous things must end.

Goodbye Paul O'Neill, Tino Martinez, Scott Brosius,
Chuck Knoblauch and David Justice. Hello Jason Giambi,
Robin Ventura, Rondell White and the other new pinstripers.

Why wait 'til next year?
The future is now.

As Roger Kahn once wrote,
"Every year is next year for the New York Yankees."

Know when it's over.

As Yogi Berra advised with indisputable logic,
"It ain't over 'til it's over." And this book is over.

• About the Author •

George Sullivan, a goldcard lifetime member of the Baseball Writers Association of America, has been writing about the major leagues in one form or another for 50 years—half the Yankees' existence.

A longtime sportswriter/columnist for the late *Boston Herald Traveler*, Sullivan joined the *Boston Globe* as a contributing writer/editor while a journalism professor at Boston University, his alma mater. He later was public relations director for the Red Sox before returning to writing books full-time.

Sullivan's stories have been featured in the *New York Times*, *Washington Post* and *USA Today*, and he has written for such magazines as *Sports Illustrated*, *Sport*, *Baseball Digest* and *Yankee*. This is his eleventh book, his third on the Yankees—co-authoring *The Yankees: An Illustrated History* with Pulitzer Prize–winner John Powers.

The ex-Marine has worn a Yankees uniform numerous times—first as visiting-team bat boy at Fenway Park during the storied summer of '49, later hand-me-down pinstripes (Johnny Kucks' shirt, Joe Pepitone's pants) while masquerading as a Yank farmhand in an Eastern League doubleheader during a George Plimpton–like adventure into participatory journalism.

A lifelong Greater Bostonian, Sullivan frequently visits the Bronx—ever since 1956, when he stopped off at Yankee Stadium on his first Red Sox road trip.